Unshakable

Unshakable

Imani L Cross

Foreword

Unshakable is more than just a book. It's a journey, a movement, a declaration that your voice matters, your work is valuable, and your identity is a strength. As you turn these pages, remember, you are not alone on this journey. Together, we can redefine the narrative and claim our space in the professional world. My father-in-law who grew up during a very racist and segregated South, subjected to a watermelon being thrown at him while he was going to school accepted and lived with the rejection and comforting himself by always saying *"I aint going where they don't want me"*. That was his way of taking back his pride whenever he felt it was being challenged.

I used to believe that and stayed out of certain neighborhoods or social circles believing that I was standing up for myself. Letting them have it sort of speak. Letting them know that my life wouldn't pause because they didn't invite me into theirs. But, as I got older and more worldly, I realized I was only hurting me. I refused to allow myself to feel thrown away by a system that didn't want me there.

Aside from my hope that this book will allow those who have not had a fair chance to feel empowered to claim their space, I encourage those who have not experienced the same struggles to read with empathy. Corporations must do more than set standard goals. They must educate their employees. Supervisors, HR professionals, and colleagues alike must remember that words, when spoken, should always preserve the dignity of others and actions should enforce that dignity in practice.

In this book, I present to you eleven transformative strategies. These are not mere theories but are the essence of my lived experiences, tailored to empower and motivate. They are designed to help you unearth the best version of yourself, to thrive in environments that may not have been designed with you in mind.

My professional background is extensive, with experience in conventional, affordable, and commercial real estate. I've undertaking years of training and gotten all the certifications and licenses needed for my profession yet, here I am, putting my experiences to paper because although I was more than qualified, I was not "certified" in their eyes.

Years of self-coaching and relentless pursuit of the right strategies have led me to where I am today. I share this journey with you, not just as an author, but as a living testament to the power of self-belief and determination. Today, I stand as the Regional Vice President of a very large company, continuing to make lateral moves and shatter glass ceilings, not just for myself, but as a beacon for others who come from backgrounds like mine.

As a woman of color my journey in the professional world has been a complex tapestry woven with threads of perseverance, resilience, and self-discovery. For many years, I dwelled in the shadows, a silent witness to the unyielding dynamics of a work environment that often seemed blind to diversity and inclusivity. Overworked, underpaid, and unappreciated, I endured a reality where my efforts, marked by countless sleepless nights, were often overshadowed by others taking credit.

The answer, a revelation in itself, came not in the form of an external validation, but as an inner awakening. My journey wasn't hindered by a lack of intelligence, qualifications, education, or experience. It was about how I perceived myself and in turn, how I presented myself to the professional world. This allowed me to be treated with much disrespect. This understanding was the catalyst for a profound transformation. I embarked on a journey of self-examination and self-motivation, discovering the immense power of self-affirmation and identity. The person I was then would be proud of the person I am today. Through immense heat and pressure, I came through as the rarest diamond.

Inside This book

Chapter 1

"Priscilla and I decided that we will handle this lease up considering the level of luxury it entails"

"I have years of experience in the luxury market and leased my first property by myself within 6 months" I confidently stated.

"Yeah, but this will take a certain level of class"

"You don't think I can lease a luxury building or have the class to do so? Why may I ask"

No valid reason was provided. Just a judgmental look whose eyes stated, you're not luxury material.

Peyton was the VP of marketing and the one who made the above comments. Peyton dresses like vibes were enough but judged me like she had a stylist on retainer. She was short and stout, and her go to outfit-a blazer and pants she seemed to rotate through the same week-was clearly not a suit. The blacks didn't match. One was faded, the other shiny. Sometimes the wrinkles in the fabric suggested she had simply air-dried it overnight and thrown it back on in the morning. It wasn't a suit. It was a compromise.

Her hair often looked either freshly washed but untouched by a comb, or like it hadn't seen water in days and left to fend for itself. Her nails were never manicured. Her flats, always scuffed, told their own tired story.

This was her everyday appearance. A woman with the title of Vice President who stated "this will take a certain level of class". Nothing about her professional appearance said "effort".

In contrast, I made a concerted effort. Fresh dry-cleaned full suits, heels that were simple, yet elegant, manicured hands and feet (though not for show) makeup applied with care and not a single strand of hair out of place.

It was in observing her appearance which was objectively less polished than mine and replaying her statement "this will take a certain level of class", I realized that I was considered inferior. Because in her mind, she deserved what she had. She owed no one the effort. And I, no matter how hard I tried, could never quite measure up.

The saddest part? I doubt her professional appearance was much different the day she interviewed for the role she now held. That my friend is what being privileged looks like. You see, despite her looking like she made no effort, I was the one being scrutinized, judged and considered to be less than. She made no attempt to hide her sense of superiority.

The above remarks and behavior went on for months until I finally called a meeting with all executives and expressed the frustration and disrespect. I was very candid about how it made me feel and how unacceptable it was. I faced the truth head on. I saw her superiority complex for what it was, an unearned sense of entitlement wrapped in condescension. I refused to let it slide.

I called it out, not with aggression, but with grace. I positioned myself to be seen, heard and respected for who I am and what I bring to the table. Silence, in moments like that, can be mistaken as acceptance and this was not the time to be silent.

This was the time to stand tall, to make it clear, to her and anyone watching, that I am educated, composed, and worthy of respect. Her title and melanin gave her no right to minimize me or question my place. I didn't stoop to her level. I rose above it and made sure everyone else saw the difference.

The individual was removed from the project, an apology issued, and boundary lines clearly drawn. I won! The policies in place worked! I broke down a major barrier! well, that is what I thought.

I found myself working with this individual again, only this time, before they started the project, I requested a meeting to set a clear understanding of what I would accept and the repercussions if the behavior did not remain professional. I didn't shy away from expressing myself. Afterall, that individual was bold enough to insult me to my face so why should I not be bold enough to stand up for myself and others who look like me.

In the words spoken by Angela Davis, 'I am no longer accepting the things I cannot change. I am changing the things I cannot accept."

Many fought and suffered for the rights that exist today. But rights, like a home, don't sustain themselves. A house may be built strong, but without regular maintenance, even the sturdiest structure begins to break down. The same is true for justice and equality, they must be actively protected, nurtured and reinforced every day. Remember, just because you made it to the chair at the table, doesn't necessarily mean everyone in the room wants you there. It will be your responsibility to not only prove that you deserve your seat and, probably some of theirs, but to make sure they view you and others who look like you with the dignity and respect they view themselves and others who look like them.

Sometimes you have to revisit an awkward, uncomfortable situation more than once before it gets resolved. When people carry deep-rooted prejudices, no citation of the law or recitation of your rights will unravel their conviction.

However, your consistency, your quiet insistence on being treated with respect and the undeniable strength of your abilities, that is what ultimately silences them.

The hope, of course, is that your presence plants a seed. A seed that leads to self-reflection and eventually, growth.

But until then, they will learn at the very least to offer you the respect and dignified treatment you've always deserved.

This can only be accomplished if you understand and acknowledge the challenges in your professional landscape. Facing the truth about your current professional environment head on is crucial. This will help determine if it's a steppingstone towards your goals or merely a stopgap.

Take some time and reflect. Ask yourself questions such as:

- What is the percentage of minority leaders in the company's hierarchy?
- How is minority representation at the leadership level compared to the overall workforce demographics?
- Are there any initiatives or programs aimed at promoting minority employees to leadership positions?
- What is the range of educational backgrounds among the leaders? (For example, do they mostly come from

    similar universities or fields of study, or is there a wide variety?)

- Does the company value diverse educational backgrounds and hands on experience in its leadership team?

- Are there leaders who have unconventional or non-traditional educational paths, demonstrating the
    company's openness to varied experiences?

- Does the company offer leadership development programs, and are these programs accessible to employees
    from various backgrounds?

- Are there mentorship or sponsorship programs in place that support employees from minority groups in
    their professional growth?

- How transparent is the company about the career paths that have led individuals to leadership roles?

- Are there case studies, profiles, or presentations where leaders share their career journeys, highlighting the
    diversity of paths and backgrounds?

- How does the company's leadership demonstrate commitment to inclusivity?

- Are leaders trained in diversity and inclusion best practices?

- Does the company's culture and policies support the inclusion and advancement of people
    from diverse backgrounds into leadership roles?

- Are there barriers or biases in the company that might impact my chances of joining the leadership team?

- Do I see traits, backgrounds, or experiences in the current leadership team that align with my own?

- Are there leaders who have taken a path similar to mine or who share my background or identity?

By incorporating these questions and areas of focus, you can more comprehensively evaluate the diversity of leadership in terms of minority representation and educational backgrounds. This assessment will help you understand the company's dedication to diversity, equity, and inclusion at all levels, particularly in its leadership roles and more importantly to YOU. Does your professional landscape have Peytons caring for the lawn?

This evaluation is not intended to cast a negative light on your employer. Rather, it's aimed at discerning whether they have, perhaps subconsciously, adhered to a mold of non-inclusivity that is unfortunately common in the workforce. It's important to recognize that many organizations may unknowingly perpetuate certain biases or exclusionary practices. By examining these aspects, we not only identify potential areas for growth but also understand how we, as individuals, can actively contribute to shaping a more inclusive and diverse workplace. It's about recognizing our own role in promoting change and taking the initiative to advocate for ourselves and others. This approach empowers each of us to be a catalyst for positive change, ensuring that our work environment is welcoming and equitable for us and those who follow.

In an article dated December 15, 2021, by Tracy Jan in The Washington Post, a significant issue within the corporate landscape of America was brought to light. The article underscored the stark disparity in racial representation at the executive level, notably pointing out the alarmingly low percentage of Black individuals in top executive positions. Furthermore, it was highlighted that those appointed to bridge this gap and foster inclusion often faced considerable challenges in making substantial progress.

Four years have passed since this article was published, and it appears that little has changed in this arena. While many corporations publicly advocate for diversity, equity, and inclusion (DEI), the necessity for specialized roles or departments such as Diversity and Inclusion Officers indicates that these values are not yet seamlessly integrated into the core operations of these organizations. The reliance on dedicated positions or departments to ensure the presence and promotion of DEI principles suggests that these efforts are more of a mandated commitment rather than a naturally occurring aspect of the corporate ethos. They need to be monitored to comply. Forced to I would say. And we all know, if someone feels forced to do something, they are not happy about it and you will feel the effects of their discontent. Some are well intended of course but the fact that the percentage of minority executives are still low unless they are self-made, reveals the feelings of the majority.

This observation raises concerns about the authenticity and depth of DEI initiatives in the corporate world. It implies that for meaningful change to occur in terms of diversity and inclusion, a fundamental shift in the corporate mindset is required - one where DEI becomes an intrinsic part of the business culture, rather than an externally imposed or superficially adopted strategy.

Simply put, a company would just see that you qualify. Nothing else if it was fair. Afterall, equality is not something that is automatic. You earn it and then protect it for those after you.

In examining your professional landscape with these insightful and probing questions, you begin the essential task of dismantling hidden barriers, biases, and systems that might otherwise hinder your journey toward success. Remember Tracy Jan's revealing article from The Washington Post (December 15, 2021), highlighting the troubling scarcity of racial diversity in executive leadership roles across corporate America. The persistence of specialized Diversity and Inclusion roles, rather than seamless integration into core company cultures, underscores the magnitude of the challenge we face. The absence of substantial progress since then signals a call to action—not just from corporations, but from you, the individual determined to redefine these spaces.

Understand that your role is not passive; you are an active participant in reshaping workplace culture. By confronting uncomfortable truths and setting clear boundaries, as illustrated by the encounter with Peyton, you reclaim your power and establish respect not only for yourself but also for those who come after you because Peyton didn't go away, she was just silenced because I didn't accept her behavior. That doesn't mean she saw her behavior as wrong, it just meant she knew she couldn't get away with expressing it at work. You have to stay vigilant and nip it in the bud.

As you move forward, carry this awareness: achieving equality is an ongoing commitment that demands courage, consistency, and clarity. It's not merely about recognizing barriers but actively breaking them down, piece by piece, encounter by encounter. Now that you have faced reality head-on, the question becomes: How do you leverage this new-found clarity to unlock your full potential? The next chapter will guide you to the pivotal next step, cultivating deep self-awareness to unleash your unshakable strength and redefine what it means to succeed. Let's explore the profound journey of self-awareness, empowering you to identify your unique strengths, acknowledge areas for growth, and cultivate an inner confidence that remains resilient regardless of external circumstances. Let's take this crucial step together, diving deeper into the key that unlocks true and lasting empowerment.

Chapter 1 Accepting Reality – Facing The Truth Head- On Self-Reflection:

1. What assumptions have you been holding onto that might be holding you back?

2. Describe a moment when you recognized a subtle or overt form of bias. How did you respond and how did it impact you?

3. What professional or personal reality have you been avoiding, and what might happen if you faced it directly?

4. In what areas of your work or life have you chosen silence? What might it look like to speak up, even if it's uncomfortable?

5. What from this chapter can you use to help yourself move forward?

6. How can you set clearer boundaries or standards for how you expect to be treated?

Chapter 2

Self-awareness is the conscious knowledge and reflection of your own personality, individuality, and abilities. In simpler terms, it means truly knowing and authentically being yourself. A lack of self-awareness can lead us to make decisions that may please others yet ultimately cause us to act in ways inconsistent with our true selves, creating discomfort and unnecessary mistakes.

I recall a pivotal moment vividly, a crucial meeting where we aimed to acquire a major asset. I was invited to attend and represent the operations team. The room was filled with 15 professionals, each prepared and composed. When it was my turn to speak, I made a critical error, I chose to leave my seat and deliver an overly animated presentation, attempting to please a team member who suggested when it was my turn that I be "engaging." As a result, I became extremely nervous, completely losing track of my thoughts and presentation. To make matters worse, I had left my carefully prepared notes at my seat.

My original message was powerful and well-crafted, but it went unheard. By trying to be someone I was not, I lost the admiration and respect of the room instantly. Although public speaking is typically one of my strengths, on this day, because I deviated from my authentic self, I failed spectacularly. The aftermath was brutal, a sleepless night, overwhelming self-doubt, and deep embarrassment.

In a corporate environment that often isn't designed with you in mind, it's essential to remember that preconceived notions of who you are may overshadow your true identity. Be prepared for unfair scrutiny but don't let it discourage you. Instead, affirm your worth regularly. After this challenging incident, I literally looked myself in the mirror and reassured myself: "You are great. You are human. You made a mistake. Time moves forward so let's make today better."

I chose not to dwell on the past but rather focused on what I had learned and how I could regain my peace of mind and power over my emotions. My first step was to apologize to my team, clearly stating I had reflected deeply and would not repeat the same mistake. I openly acknowledged why I behaved as I did and reassured them it would not recur.

I soon had the opportunity to prove my words. The company invited us back for a second presentation, this time to their entire board and it's supporters. I now had an audience of over 100 people instead of 15. I prepared diligently. When it was my turn to speak, I deliberately did not look at the team member who suggested I "be more engaging." Instead, I focused on the audience and, most importantly, stayed true to myself. This presentation was a success and we won the contract. I regained my confidence and credibility.

Self-awareness helps you remain grounded during stressful moments and guides your decision-making process. By understanding your strengths, weaknesses, emotions, and motivations, you can better navigate professional and personal challenges. Self-aware individuals tend to communicate more effectively, resolve conflicts productively, and maintain healthier relationships in all areas of their lives. They possess greater emotional intelligence, which is crucial in environments where empathy, understanding, and effective interaction with colleagues are highly valued.

Furthermore, self-awareness allows for authentic leadership. When you clearly understand who you are and what you stand for, your confidence naturally shines through, and others recognize and respect your authenticity. Leaders who embrace self-awareness inspire trust, foster open communication, and create environments where team members feel valued and empowered. Authenticity in leadership isn't about perfection; it's about transparency, consistency, and vulnerability.

Additionally, self-awareness is integral to personal growth. Being aware of your personal biases, limitations, and areas for improvement provides a clear roadmap for continuous development. It enables you to identify opportunities for learning and growth proactively. Instead of fearing criticism or setbacks, a self-aware individual views these situations as opportunities for improvement and as stepping stones toward greater resilience and success.

Like that teammate, some people may offer advice with good intentions, but unless it's task-specific such as guidance on creating a report, you should listen respectfully and then determine if their suggestion aligns with your authentic self. I had a supervisor who, after each presentation, pointed out my "pregnant pauses" and "nervous energy." Yet the audience consistently complimented my delivery and highlighted the valuable points I had made. I was fully aware of how I prepared my presentation and what I said but that supervisors comment would discourage me. The reaction of the audience however, and the questions after, told a different story. They enjoyed, actively listened and were engaged. Knowing this and being honest with myself, I could disagree with that supervisor. Being self-aware allowed me to discern constructive feedback from potentially harmful criticism. Ultimately, if you aren't honest with yourself, you'll find it difficult to identify when others are genuinely honest with you which can cause you to find yourself in unnecessary difficult situations.

Embrace your self-awareness. It is your most reliable guide in navigating life's complexities, enhancing your emotional intelligence, and achieving lasting success. Trust in your abilities, remain authentic, and continuously strive to understand and develop yourself. This is how you unleash your true potential.

Chapter 2 Self-Awareness – The Key To Unleashing Potential- Self Reflection

1. When have you acted out of character to meet someone else's expectations?

2. What strengths do you undervalue in yourself and why?

3. Think of a recent mistake. What did it teach you about your growth edge?

4. How can you create daily habits that reconnect you with your authentic self?

Chapter 3

Tripple .... she said casually. That's what my son calls them.

There was a silence. The kind of silence that isn't just quiet but heavy, suffocating. It felt like an eternity. Then, as if to soften the blow, she added: "But... you're not like them. You're different."

The words were jarring not just because of their content, but because of who said them.

This came from a colleague who, ironically, oversaw all of our legal cases. Her name was Melanie.

Melanie was a middle-aged Caucasian and had been with the firm for over twenty years. She always seemed composed and kind. Someone who gave off the impression of being friendly, reasonable, and professional. Her tone was usually controlled, her manner unflappable. She wasn't flashy or loud, and her steady presence often made her a go-to for guidance.

She also had a very clear, very visible crush on the company's owner. In meetings, she would pepper her updates with unsolicited compliments toward him, usually about how well he handled a call or how sharp he looked in a particular tie. It was always said with a grin, always lighthearted but enough to make him visibly blush, every time.

Melanie wasn't someone you'd expect that kind of comment from. And maybe that's what made it worse. There was no anger in her voice, no ill will in her tone. Just casual prejudice dressed up as a compliment. The kind of bias that hides behind familiarity and smiles.

And it wasn't just casual, it was deep-rooted and recent. The moment she said, "That's what my son calls them," it struck me like a punch to the chest. That wasn't just a slip of the tongue or an outdated phrase. It was active language, passed down, used in her home. That told me everything I needed to know.

She and her family were living proof of an old, painful truth: they probably call us .... at their dinner table.

This phrase isn't just a bitter assumption but a defense mechanism, a whispered truth passed among people of color to explain the unspoken hostility we often feel but can't always prove. It's a way of naming the tension between how we're treated in public with the polite smiles, performative alliance and the suspicion that behind closed doors, the real feelings emerge. Feelings that reduce us to stereotypes, slurs, and caricatures.

It's not said to be cynical, but to stay alert. To be reminded that racism isn't always loud or obvious. Sometimes it's subtle, a tone, a glance, a decision made in a meeting. But Melanie's comment made it plain. She didn't just confirm the suspicions, she embodied them. Her words weren't just a slip; they were a window into the private conversations we're rarely allowed to hear.

And in that moment, I realized: the things we've always feared are not imagined. They're real. They're sitting across from us at the conference table, handling our legal cases and smiling all while thinking we don't belong, and we are nothing.

They go home and, over dinner, mock our names, our voices, our presence. They reduce us then they rinse their dishes, tuck their children into bed, and prepare for the next day—ready to perform professionalism again. To offer polite smiles, to feign inclusivity all while thinking the worst of us.

This duality is not uncommon. As highlighted in discussions about private racism, many individuals harbor prejudiced views that they express in private settings, even as they maintain a facade of tolerance in public spheres.

This duplicity is exhausting. It's the unspoken weight we carry into every meeting, review, and networking event. It's the knowledge that behind the veneer of corporate civility lies a truth we've always known but rarely hear confirmed: that to them, we are outsiders, tolerated, but never truly accepted.

And in that moment, I realized she really was doing that.

Right there in the middle of a professional exchange, after I had just spent the day representing our company in court, securing a legal victory, upholding my responsibility with grace and professionalism, this is what she chose to say. That was her takeaway.

Let me explain how we got there.

At the time, I was handling a particularly difficult case involving a resident who was a habitual late payer and had become increasingly combative. We had gone to court multiple times, and the situation had reached a point where I was asked to appear in court with our attorney to represent management.

From a poor attempt at mediation to awaiting trial, the day was grueling.

We sat for hours while the tenant offered misleading statements, twisted truths, and leveled accusations one after the other. I had to sit in silence, bite my tongue, and wait for our moment to respond. I knew the facts. I knew our paperwork was solid. I knew we were in the right. But still, the waiting, the restraint, the quiet professionalism, it wore on me.

Finally, the judge ruled in our favor. The gavel dropped, and justice prevailed. It should have felt like a victory.

So, I called Melanie to update her on the outcome. I expected a "Great job," or even just a "Thanks for the update."

Instead, I got:

"Triple ....". That's what my son calls them. But you're not like them."

I was stunned. My heart raced. My hands clenched. That victory, so hard-fought, suddenly felt tainted. What should have been a celebration turned into a stark reminder of where I stood in her eyes, not as a professional who won a difficult case, but as an exception to a deeply offensive stereotype.

What hurt most wasn't just the words, it was the implication. That there's a category of people, defined by nothing more than the color of their skin, who are somehow "less than." And that I was being praised not for my work, not for my composure, but for not being "like them."

At that moment, I realized my silence would've made her comfortable, but it would've cost me something far greater, my self-respect.

This moment was a turning point.

It reminded me that silence can be a dangerous accomplice. That professionalism does not mean passivity. That breaking the silence, especially when it's uncomfortable, is often the only path to real change.

Although I knew in that moment that her feelings were deep rooted and there wouldn't be any conversion taking place, the fire within me burned to speak. So I did. I didn't raise my voice that day. I didn't lash out. But I did speak up. Calmly, clearly, and without apology. I reminded Melanie that her words were not just inappropriate, they were deeply offensive. I explained that "being different" should not be a compliment when the standard is built on prejudice. I let her know that I wouldn't allow silence to be mistaken for agreement.

And just like that, the awkwardness shifted from mine to hers. Rightfully so.

This chapter of my life and this chapter in this book is not just about calling out racism or ignorance. It's about finding your voice when everything around you says, "Stay quiet." It's about reclaiming power in spaces where others may try to strip it away with a smile and a microaggression.

Speaking up doesn't always feel triumphant. Often, it's draining. Risky and Lonely but it's also necessary.

When you find your voice, you don't just speak for yourself, you speak for those who can't, those who won't, and those who are still learning how. You create space for truth. For growth. For equity.

Because silence might keep the peace but your voice will change the culture so you HAVE to speak up.

And I did. Not only to Melanie, but to the owner as well. I brought the comment to his attention and expressed how insulting and inappropriate it was not just to me, but to what we claimed to stand for as a company.

He tried to dismiss it. Brushed it off, really. His response was diluted by his long-standing familiarity with Melanie, and that unspoken tendency many people have. They'll say they believe in equality, they'll nod during the diversity training, but when the moment calls for action, when it's time to confront, correct, or do something, they retreat into discomfort. They shy away.

I don't even blame him, honestly. I had worked with him for years. He was always... spineless. A "yes" person. The kind of leader who preferred to avoid problems instead of resolve them. He lived by the unspoken motto: "That's what I pay you for."

But here's the irony, the person he was paying was the very one exposing him to risk. Comments like Melanie's could cost the company dearly. But this wasn't that kind of firm. It was small. Tight-knit. Loyal to tenure, not truth. Melanie wasn't going anywhere.

So what did my speaking up do?

It didn't trigger an investigation. There was no HR memo, no grand disciplinary meeting. Nothing "happened" to Melanie.

But here's the truth: sometimes breaking the silence won't change the system overnight.

Sometimes, it won't even change the room. But, it will change you.

Speaking up in a world that often punishes truth-tellers can feel like shouting into the void. You may not receive applause or immediate validation. In fact, you might face resistance, isolation, or even retaliation. Research indicates that oppression based on race and other identities predicts poor mental health, with increased exposure to discrimination leading to higher rates of depression and anxiety among marginalized groups .

Yet, choosing to speak out is an act of reclaiming your power. It's a declaration that your experiences and voice matter. As noted by the National Equity Project, understanding the impact of systemic oppression is crucial in recognizing how it hinders progress and perpetuates inequality .

In this reality, where systems are slow to change, your voice becomes a catalyst not just for external transformation, but for personal empowerment. It's a step toward breaking the cycle of silence and fostering a sense of self-worth and resilience.

Your presence will be felt. Your dignity will not be challenged any further. The next time you walk into that meeting, people will think twice. Their words will be more cautious. Their jokes will fall quiet before they form.

And yes, at times, it may leave you feeling upset. Unheard. Alone.

But trust me, that shift in the conversation, that hesitation before they speak, that new awareness, they now know better. And whether they admit it or not, you were the reason why.

I've since left that company and truthfully, it's still the same. Same workers. Same mindset. The same small culture where tenure often trumps transformation. No one ever really held Melanie accountable. And they probably never will.

But I moved on and with every lateral move I've made, I've discovered something far more valuable than a title, I've found my voice. I've been elevated several times since then, even being honored for my distinguished service at a recent company event and Melanie, I couldn't tell you because nothing she's done has had any notoriety.

The benefits? I found new Melanies too. They always show up eventually. But the difference now is, I know exactly how to handle them. I know how to recognize those microaggressions before they're even fully spoken. I know how to respond without losing my peace. I know how to maintain my professionalism while protecting my dignity, my mental well-being, and just as critically my monetary contribution to my family because, standing up for yourself shouldn't mean sacrificing your livelihood. It should mean honoring it and I also know when to leave and not grace them with my presence.

This chapter isn't just about confrontation. It's about responsibility. Power. Purpose.

The responsibility to model strength for those watching.
The power that comes from not shrinking in the face of injustice.
And the purpose of using your voice not for vengeance, but for visibility.

Every time you speak up with courage and composure, you make the workplace a little less comfortable for bigotry, and a little more livable for those like you. You shift the narrative. You disrupt the default. You draw a line that cannot be erased.

And that, in itself, is a legacy worth building.

How to Protect Your Peace While Using Your Voice?

Know when to speak and when to document. Not every battle needs to be verbal. Some require a paper trail.

Respond, don't react. Power is in composure. Calm doesn't mean compliant, it means in control.

Say what needs to be said then move forward. Don't waste energy trying to educate those committed to misunderstanding you.

Create allies where you can, but never depend on them to validate your experience. Your truth is yours.

Remember, silence isn't safety, It's invisibility. Speak so they can't say they didn't know.

Melanies exist in every workplace. Sometimes they wear pearls, sometimes they wear hoodies. What they all have in common is the ability to smile while shrinking you unless you speak.

Let the next room you walk into know that your silence is no longer available. Your presence will speak even louder than your words.

Chapter 3 Breaking The Silence – Finding Your Voice- Self Reflection

1. What's one moment when you stayed silent and later wished you hadn't?

2. What fears come up for you when you think about speaking truth in professional spaces?

3. How do you decide when to confront, when to document, and when to disengage?

4. Who do you need to speak up for, besides yourself?

Chapter 4

I used to think I needed permission. Permission to lead. Permission to speak. Permission to be seen.

That belief didn't come from nowhere. It came from years of subtle cues such as being overlooked in meetings, praised for how well I "handled myself" but rarely given a seat at the decision table, told to "wait my turn," even when I knew I was the most qualified person in the room. It became so ingrained that I found myself doing something I hadn't done since childhood, literally raising my hand to ask to speak in meetings.

What is Self-Doubt?

Self-doubt is a lack of confidence in yourself and your abilities. It's the inner critic that second-guesses your qualifications, undermines your successes, and keeps you in a cycle of hesitation. It's the voice that asks, "Are you sure you belong here?" even when your résumé, your results, and your reputation say yes.

You see, the most persistent voice you'll ever hear isn't your supervisor's. It isn't even your critic's. It's your own.

Self-doubt whispers louder than outside judgment. It tells you you're not ready. That if you mess up, everyone will notice. That if you speak boldly, you'll come off too strong. That success is for someone else. Someone more polished, more connected, more perfect.

And because that voice sounds like yours, you believe it.

I know I did.

Self-doubt can deplete your strength without ever laying a hand on you. It tells you not to even try. It creates a completely false narrative and then convinces you it's the truth.

It'll make you believe no one likes you when in reality, they admire you.
It tells you that you sounded foolish when you spoke when your audience actually hung on to every word.

It conditions you to seek constant affirmation asking if you did okay, fishing for compliments, waiting for others to tell you that you're good enough just so you can feel better about yourself.

Self-doubt disables motivation because that's exactly what it is, you doubting yourself, your ability, your worth, your value.

No matter how many people cheer you on or reassure you of your greatness, it won't matter if you can't see it for yourself. You'll second-guess every move. You'll rewrite emails ten times. You'll dissect every presentation. You'll replay every conversation.

It is EXHAUSTING.

In the beginning of my leadership role, I found myself doing just that. After calls, I'd follow up with peers or colleagues, asking: "How did I do?"
I wasn't doing it for growth or improvement. I was doing it for approval.
I just needed someone to say, "Great job."

It was the wrong reason and I had to stop.

I had to learn how to believe in my abilities, the same way others did. I needed to develop the confidence I projected on the outside and actually own it on the inside. I needed to respect myself the way others already respected me.

That's where self-awareness helped.

Understanding and admitting the truth about myself helped me recognize this trait for what it was, a pattern. And like any pattern, once you see it clearly, you can start working to change it. That moment of clarity set me on a course to begin overcoming my internal barriers.

This doesn't mean I never feel doubt anymore. This isn't a "fix-all" strategy. You are human and an imperfect one at that. You will have days when you question yourself, your decisions, or your effectiveness. That's normal. But the difference now is that I can identify it. I can pause and say, "This isn't truth. This is insecurity. And I don't need to answer to it today."

How Self-Doubt Shows Up at Work.

You pass on opportunities because you assume someone else is more qualified.

You over-explain simple decisions, fearing others won't trust your judgment.

You delay leadership by waiting for a "perfect" moment that never comes.

You avoid visibility, letting others present your work while you hide in the background.

You reject compliments, downplaying your own success to seem "humble" when it's really discomfort in receiving praise.

You self-sabotage, procrastinating on big tasks because you secretly fear you won't execute them well.

Sometimes, self-doubt doesn't sound like "I'm not good enough." Sometimes, it sounds more like, "Let me just double check one more time."

Or, "I don't want to bother anyone."

Or, "They probably already know that."

These thoughts seem harmless—but over time, they chip away at your confidence, your momentum, and your growth.

When I Chose to Believe in Myself.

I remember my very first budget presentation in my current role. It was the first time I had to speak directly to a formal audience. Just me at the front of the room, presenting to owners, investors, asset managers, and financial analysts who knew the financial lingo far better than I did.

And it wasn't just one presentation. It was four in one day.

I had one month to prepare, and some of the attendees I had never even met. It would be their first time seeing me in action. Their first impression. That pressure sat heavy on my shoulders, and as the day drew closer, my nervousness grew. I practiced relentlessly. It's hard to rehearse for the unknown. The fear of being caught off guard was intense.

The day before the presentations, my supervisor reached out and asked me to go over it with her. After I walked her through my material, she looked at me and said, "You're ready. Just keep in mind they may ask you something you don't know. Don't pretend to know it. Just speak on what you do know."

The next day, I sat in the waiting room at the office, awaiting my turn. My heart was pounding so loud I could hear it. I took several deep breaths. I whispered to myself, "No turning back now. Just go in and do your best." And I did.

One thing I've learned is that sometimes, the audience can unintentionally make things harder. Their own insecurities may surface in the form of challenging questions, often aimed at proving their own credibility to the room. That's okay. Don't let it shake you. Stay calm, focus on your material, and know that it's perfectly acceptable to revisit a question later if you don't have an immediate answer as stated by my supervisor.

You might tell yourself you can't do it but you can. Give yourself that grace. Stay focused.

The presentations, which totaled nearly two hours, went exceptionally well. I received warm feedback, compliments on my delivery, and most importantly, a genuine welcome to my role. It went so well that the team decided to invest in my growth by enrolling me in specialized training to prepare me for a more senior position. I'm still taking those courses now, growing more confident and capable with each passing module.

That entire month of preparation, without a formal outline or template, became an affirmation of my own capabilities and that is important in order to shrink self-doubt.

I knew my properties. I understood their financial health. Rather than sit in self-doubt, I took action. I researched. I called our financial analysts and asked questions. I looked through prior PowerPoints from previous leaders and compared each asset's performance from then to now. I saw with my own eyes the evidence of my leadership. The needle was moving in the right direction.

That's when it hit me, I am the right person for this job. And it was time they saw that too.

If I had listened to the doubtful voice, the one that said, you're not ready, you're going to fail, you don't belong in that room, I would've sat back, waited for more help, and gone in unprepared. That one day of review with my supervisor, helpful as it was, would never have been enough. The truth is, I helped myself. I coached myself through it. This is not meant to sound arrogant, but to convey the message, that being self-motivated is important. You can't always rely on others. You need to help yourself.

That's the part of self-belief people don't always talk about. It doesn't come in the moment of performance, it comes from every decision you make before the moment. Every time you decide to try. To prepare. To trust your instincts. To show up.

And the lesson? I didn't need to feel completely confident to be competent. I just needed to act on what I knew and give myself a chance to prove that I was already enough.

Closing Reflection: How to Rebuild Self-Belief

Keep a record of your wins. Big or small, write them down. Progress becomes visible when tracked.

Separate facts from feelings. Just because you feel unsure doesn't mean you're unqualified.

Ask yourself: "Would I question someone else in my position?" If the answer is no, give yourself the same grace.

Practice in private, perform with presence. Your preparation builds your confidence long before you speak.

Celebrate effort, not just outcomes. The process of showing up and trying matters.

Affirm your growth. You're not who you were a year ago. Remind yourself of that often.

Self-belief isn't about thinking you're perfect. It's about knowing that you're capable even when you feel afraid. It's not arrogance. It's alignment. It's understanding your value and giving yourself permission to show it.

The power to silence self-doubt isn't something you wait to be given. It's something you decide to take back.

And when you do, there's no limit to how far you'll go.

Chapter 4 The Power Of Self-Belief – Overcoming Internal Barriers- Self Reflection

1. What voice of self-doubt has been the loudest for you lately?

2. Where in your life are you still asking for permission to be great?

3. Describe a time when you proved your own value through action. What did that teach you?

4. How will you practice affirming your worth before others recognize it?

Chapter 5

Sometimes you feel stuck in your current role and not because you lack talent or ambition, but because the circumstances around you seem immovable. Maybe it's the financial necessity that keeps you rooted. A stable paycheck, benefits, or job security can make even a toxic work environment feel like a burden you're forced to carry. For others, it's geography. Your job is close to home, your children's school, or a sick relative you're caring for. The thought of relocating or adding hours to your commute feels overwhelming.

Sometimes you're stuck because the market is tight. You've applied for dozens of positions, only to receive rejection after rejection or worse, silence. You may even find roles that match your skills perfectly, only to learn they've hired internally or favored someone with a referral.

You might also feel stuck because of fear. Fear that if you leave, you won't find better. Fear that starting over means starting at the bottom. Fear that your next opportunity might look different, but feel the same.

And then there's the emotional toll. When you've been passed over, undervalued, or dismissed enough times, you begin to second-guess your worth. You question if you're really "ready." You stay not because you're content but because you've been conditioned to survive discomfort rather than demand better.

There's no clear map for career growth especially not when you come from a background that doesn't match the blueprint of the traditional corporate ladder. Advancement often looks less like a straight line and more like a labyrinth. A winding, deliberate path designed to test your endurance more than your intelligence.

A labyrinth isn't just a maze. It's a complex structure designed to confuse, mislead, and test your persistence. The walls are high. The turns are sharp. There's no clear signage, no guide, and oftentimes, no indication of whether you're getting closer to the center or just circling around.

In the corporate world, the labyrinth takes form in subtler ways such as unspoken rules about who gets visibility.

The Labyrinth Isn't a Coincidence. It's a System.

Corporate America often frames success as a simple formula. Show up, work hard, get rewarded. But for many of us, the path forward is anything but straightforward. It doesn't resemble a staircase or even a maze with clues. It feels more like a labyrinth.

A labyrinth isn't just complex. It's designed to confuse. Its twisted corridors and hidden turns are built with one purpose, to disorient. And that's exactly what the corporate system does to people who were never meant to thrive within it. It gives the illusion of movement while keeping you in cycles, chasing visibility, chasing opportunity, chasing validation. But never quite arriving.

This design is not accidental.

It's reinforced by
   - Gatekeepers who smile at your ambition but never open doors
 - Systems that reward tenure over talent
 - Evaluation processes that penalize you for being too bold, too quiet,

too "different"

The result? A constant sense of being tested, but never taught. Of being watched, but not welcomed.

Mental Fortitude Is Your Way Out.

To escape a labyrinth like this, you need more than just direction. You need clarity of self. It's your mental fortitude that will become your compass. The ability to recognize that you're in a trap is the first act of liberation.

The second? Resilience.

Because once you see it for what it is, you'll need the strength to resist the pull of comfort. The voices that say, "Be patient, it'll come." The subtle rewards that try to convince you the maze is worth staying in. They are designed to keep you dependable, not powerful. And the more powerful you become, the more you threaten the illusion of fairness that the system was built on.

But when you activate your power of reason, when you stop internalizing the structure's failure as your own, you begin to build your exit strategy.

You realize that it's not that you weren't strong enough. It's that the system hoped you wouldn't notice the walls were built to keep you in. Those walls come in many designs such as, selective access to mentorship or leadership pipelines, hidden expectations that shift depending on who's in the room, gatekeepers who smile in your face while quietly blocking your path.

And just like the mythological version, this labyrinth can feel like it was never meant for you to escape. But people do. We do. Not by chance but by strategy, self-awareness, and learning when to pivot, pause, or push forward.

This chapter is about exactly that, how to stop surviving the system and start navigating it.

The trap isn't always physical either. It's mental, emotional, and systemic and unless you recognize it, name it, and develop a strategy to move through it, you'll keep telling yourself, "Maybe next year," while the years pass and nothing changes.

Because in this world, hard work is expected. It's assumed. But advancement? That's for those who learn how to move with intention.

Those who read the landscape and are not bothered by the Peytons caring for the lawn.

Those who chart their own way forward even when the walls keep shifting.

Those who break through the barriers built by outdated systems, paralyzing Melanies, and yes, even your own self-doubt that try to hold you back.

This is the chapter where you stop waiting for an open door and start building your own.

When the Maze Tried to Break Me and I Found the Exit Anyway.

There's more to the firm where I was introduced to the real Melanie.

As mentioned before, nothing changed for her. She continued to move through the workplace untouched and unbothered. But for me? Everything changed. And not in the way it should have.

I was given more work presented under the guise of a promotion but with no additional staff, no increase in support, and no relief from my existing responsibilities. What sounded like elevation was actually exploitation in a new outfit.

Late nights turned into normal hours. Weekends became extensions of my work week. I was drowning in expectations that no one else was being held to.

I asked for help, For real, ongoing support. What I got were temporary assistants who, by the time they were properly trained, the assignments would be over. I requested updated software to eliminate handwritten calculations that were slowing me down and increasing the risk of error. My request was met with enthusiasm, a presentation proposal and nothing more. Nothing ever approved.

Time wore on, and so did I. I became exhausted, overwhelmed, and eventually, I made a mistake. Not because I was careless, but because I had been overworked and denied the tools I needed to succeed.

And how was that moment handled?

The "spineless" owner, the one who had repeatedly ignored the red flags and failed to support me, finally found his voice. But he didn't use it to advocate or reflect. He used it to yell. To raise his voice at me in front of Melanie. To embarrass me publicly while conveniently ignoring the months of unpaid emotional labor and my repeated requests for support.

That was the breaking point.

I stood up calmly, but firmly. I told him directly to change his tone. I told him it was clear we had reached the end of our working relationship and that I advised him to start looking for my replacement.

He was shocked. He immediately tried to backpedal. His tone changed. His posture softened. He offered half-measures in real time. But it was too late.

That happened on a Monday.

By Wednesday, I had reached out to a recruiter and interviewed for a new role.

By Friday, I signed an offer letter for a position that elevated me in title, salary, and scope.

Within one week, the labyrinth I thought I was stuck in revealed its exit signs.

Two weeks later, I walked out. And I never looked back.

Many replacements came after me and left. It's been years, and no one has ever filled that role the way I did. That, too, is part of the story.

Find the Exit then Use It.

If you're stuck in a labyrinth, remember this, you knew where the entrance was. It's still there and it can also be your way out.

Don't just look forward. Remember the steps you took. Don't forget what led you there.

Always have an exit strategy and don't take longer than needed to use it.

The longer you stay in a bad environment, the longer it will take you to find that right match. The one that challenges you, rewards you, and respects you.

And let's be clear, I've never seen an uncut or ungroomed labyrinth. If the caretakers are putting that much effort into keeping it neat and disorienting, it's because they're investing in your confusion.

Outwit them at their own game.

Walk through the turf maze if you have to but get out.

The idea is not to help you find the way. The idea is to keep you in there. Get out on your own and don't go back. But if you can, help others avoid the trap.

Chapter 5 Navigating The Labyrinth – Strategies For Professional Advancement- Self Reflection

1. What systems or structures have made your growth feel like a maze?

2. How can you begin identifying patterns or obstacles that keep repeating?

3. What would a personal "exit strategy" from a toxic professional environment look like for you?

4. Who can help you strategize, not just survive your next move?

Chapter 6

Y̵ou can be brilliant. Strategic. Unshakably self-aware.

But even the most capable among us cannot climb alone. There's a saying that goes, "If you help someone climb a mountain, you're both standing at the top."

That's what real mentorship and support do, they lift everyone. True growth doesn't happen in isolation. Success, especially in spaces not built for you requires community. Not just the performative kind, but the kind that holds you up when you're questioning everything, opens doors when yours have been locked, and tells you the truth even when it's uncomfortable.

We hear the words mentorship and networking thrown around often, but just so there's no misunderstanding, not everyone in your circle is a supporter and not everyone offering "guidance" is actually there to help you grow.

Some people are mentors. Others are monitors. Allow me to elaborate.

Mentors vs. Monitors

A mentor invests in your potential. They give you tools, share their own failures, and want to see you surpass even their own milestones.

A monitor, on the other hand, simply watches. They may appear helpful, but their true intent is control, not development. They track your movements, critique your decisions, and offer advice that's more about keeping you in line than lifting you upward. These are the ones grooming the labyrinth to ensure you don't get out or succeed.

Mentors say, "Here's how I did it and here's what I learned when I failed."

Monitors say, "You're not ready yet."

Mentors are secure in your shine.

Monitors fear it.

Learning the difference early on can be the key to building a support system that actually supports you.

When I Met a True Mentor and Survived a Monitor.

He wasn't the approachable type. Quiet but guarded. Always well dressed, he carried himself with precision. You could smell his cologne before he entered the room. Clean, crisp, and commanding. His appearance was always neat, from the perfect knot in his tie to the polished shoes on his feet. He had an aura of excellence that didn't need to announce itself.

I didn't meet him first. My first day, I sat down with the accountant and asked the most important question I could think of:

What are some of the financial challenges at the sites? Anything specific that needs my immediate attention?

"The water bill is out of control. I can't make sense of the spikes and no one has addressed it" he replied without hesitation but clear frustration.

I took that on immediately. It became my first assignment.

I gathered every bill. I checked whether they were actual readings or estimates. I walked every unit in this community which was comprised of hundreds of units, searching for leaks. For weeks, we came up short. But I didn't give up. I knew something was wrong, and I was determined to find it.

Then, about a month in, one of my maintenance technicians called me and said, "I think we finally found that leak." It was a broken pipe that was leaking for months. The water company was contacted, the pipe was fixed, and just like that, problem solved.

The news traveled fast. Corporate heard about it almost immediately.

Then came the phone call.

"Thank you. You didn't give up. Come to my office tomorrow so we can get to know each other better."

That's when the mentoring began. He saw in me someone who cared about more than just showing up. He saw someone who cared about the investment, about the people, about the systems. Because I showed concern for what mattered to him, he chose to invest in me.

That's where our journey began and it never stopped.

After leaving the yes mannequin, I stepped into a new role full of excitement and hope. For the first time, I was paid what I was worth and given the autonomy to lead a team without being micromanaged or stifled. The owner of the company trusted me, truly trusted me and with that came one success after another.

He invested in me, gave me tools, sat me down and trained me on financials in a way that made sense to how I process information. He brought me into construction meetings and didn't just include me but asked for my input. He entrusted me with the entire company portfolio, and no major decision happened without my feedback.

He taught me how to identify the right candidates for roles, how to trust my gut, and most importantly, how to separate emotion from leadership decisions. If a person wasn't the right fit, I learned how to release them without being consumed by guilt. He even encouraged me to think beyond the job. He introduced me to his personal investment broker to ensure I was building a strong financial future of my own.

This man had photos with presidents and world leaders hanging on his office wall, but you'd never hear him brag. You only knew of those moments if you were in his office and happened to look up. He was that humble. Precise in his decision-making, fair in his compensation, and clear in his expectations.

He was a mentor. A real one.

But where there is mentorship, *there can also be monitoring*.

His relative, Helen, was the company's head of compliance. She was a monitor. Disgruntled. Cold. She operated in the shadows, often sitting in her office with the lights off. She wanted the recognition he gave others and resented anyone who received it. When attention wasn't on her, she became a silent saboteur and unfortunately, I became her target.

We were working on a project that required over 100 units to be leased under a very specific and unfamiliar program. I had never worked with this program before, and though I was supposed to be in an oversight role, I quickly found myself in the weeds and having to learn how to process the files and fast.

Then things got strange.

A member of her team showed up for a "site visit," the next day after I was asked to take on this role and suddenly all the guidance and project documentation *disappeared*. My emails went unanswered. My calls went straight to voicemail. The on-site team joined the silent resistance. It was clear I wasn't just being monitored. I was being *isolated*.

But here's the thing, mentors teach you to adapt, to lead and to *move in silence if you have to*.

I called a trusted friend in the industry and explained the sensitivity of the situation. That call led me to someone high up in the department that oversaw the very program we were dealing with. They connected me to the local field office. Their team came out, trained me, and gave me everything I needed to do the job right.

I didn't make noise. I made *progress*.

I brought in a third-party compliance team. They reviewed and approved files independently. When Helen tried to discredit me, I submitted a file along with her findings to the program administrators and received formal documentation stating that her "findings" were unfounded and opinion-based, not reflective of actual program regulations.

There was nothing the monitor could do.

When the lease-up was complete, and I met the deadline *on time and in full compliance*, she finally looked at me and said, *"You know what you're doing."*

The words were small but the resentment behind them was enormous. That sentence didn't just admit success. It *confirmed* her fear, that I had proven her oversight obsolete.

You see, mentors are always watching waiting for your next great move so they can cheer for you.

Monitors are watching too but only in hopes you slip, so they won't be revealed.

The Emotional Currency of Support.

Support in professional spaces isn't just about titles, job referrals, or who can get you into which room. That's surface-level networking. What truly fuels growth is *emotional currency* the energy, presence, and intention people are willing to share with you.

It's the colleague who checks in on you after a hard meeting.
It's the leader who gives you space to fail and room to try again.
It's the mentor who doesn't just share advice but perspective, patience, and belief.

Support is emotional. It requires trust. It takes consistency.

That's why some people, even with powerful positions, can feel empty as mentors. They're unwilling to spend the emotional currency required to help someone rise. They hoard their access. They gatekeep their journey. They see your ambition as competition instead of a continuation of the path.

Here's how you know someone is giving you real support:

- They correct you without belittling you.
- They speak your name in rooms you haven't entered yet.
- They remind you who you are when you start to forget.
- They celebrate your growth even when it surpasses their own.
- They ask you how you're doing and wait for the real answer.

Support isn't performative, it's *present*. It doesn't just say, *"Let me know if you need anything."* It says, *"Here's what I can do to help. What do you need from me right now?"*

And you can feel the difference. One energizes you. The other drains you.

Building an Authentic Network.

You don't need to collect business cards. You need to build *connections*. Real networking is less about volume and more about alignment and finding people who reflect your values, challenge your thinking, and add fuel to your mission, not friction.

Here are strategies to build a network that supports *who you are*, not just what you do:

Start with Mutual Respect, Not Mutual Benefit.

If your first thought when meeting someone is "What can they do for me?" pause. Shift the question to "Is there mutual respect here?" If the answer is yes, *then* explore the possibility of shared opportunities.

Invest Where the Energy Feels Right.

If the vibe is off, don't force it. Just because someone is successful doesn't mean they're safe. Pay attention to how people make you feel after you interact with them. *refreshed or reduced*?

Be Curious, Not Just Career-Focused.

When building connections, lead with curiosity. Ask thoughtful questions. Take genuine interest. People remember how you made them feel, not just your title or resume.

Reciprocate Without Keeping Score.

Support people without expectation. Share a job lead. Make an introduction. Offer encouragement. But don't turn it into a transaction. Generosity in networking often returns to you but not always from where you gave it.

Know Your Boundaries.

Networking doesn't mean overextending yourself. Know when to step back from draining connections or over-committing to people who never show up for you.

Build Across, Not Just Up.

Everyone wants access to the top but some of your strongest allies will be *your peers*. Build laterally. Today's co-manager could be tomorrow's executive partner.

Make Room for Mentorship—and Be One.

While you're seeking guidance, remember you also have something to offer. Share your journey. Lift as you climb. Empower someone who's navigating a path you've already walked. Show them they are not alone.

Your Circle Is Your Strategy.

At every stage of your career, you will find yourself asking:

Who's really in my corner?

Who do I trust to guide me, not judge me?

Who sharpens me without trying to shape me into something I'm not?

The answers to those questions don't just determine how supported you feel, they often determine how far you'll go.

Your circle is more than community, it's *strategy*. The right people will push you, not pressure you and aside from speaking your name in rooms you didn't even know existed, they'll remind you of your worth when the world gets too loud. They'll give you space to lead, fall, and rise again.

But most importantly, they'll let you be *you*. That authentic self we spoke about earlier.

So, build carefully. Invest wisely. Don't just network, *connect*. And when you find your people, show up for them the way you needed someone to show up for you.

Always remember, no one climbs alone and if you help someone reach the top of the mountain, *you're both standing side by side at the mountaintop.*

Chapter 6 Mentorship And Networking – Building Your Support System- Self Reflection

1. Who in your current circle genuinely supports your growth and who simply observes?

2. What barriers have you experienced in building a professional network?

3. Reflect on a time you wished for a mentor. What would you have asked for?

4. How can you distinguish between mentors and monitors in your life right now?

Chapter 7

There comes a point in every professional journey when you're no longer just doing the work, you're being seen for it. Or at least, you should be.

But visibility doesn't always come naturally. Especially not in rooms that weren't designed for your presence. Especially not when your voice, your style, or your background doesn't match the norm.

As a Regional Vice President, I've learned firsthand that leadership isn't just about the title. It's about how you show up, how you speak up, and how you stay grounded in who you are even when you're the only one in the room who looks, leads, or thinks like you.

Sometimes, you'll have to make your presence known. Other times, you'll have to remind people why you're in the room in the first place.

Claiming your space in leadership isn't about arrogance, it's about clarity in who you are and what you stand for. It's recognizing that your value doesn't decrease because others don't understand it. It's knowing that your voice carries weight, and it deserves to be heard even if it shakes. It's learning how to advocate for yourself without apologizing for your existence.

What is Self-Promotion?

Self-promotion is not bragging. It's truth-telling with intention.

It's the strategic act of sharing your skills, accomplishments, and impact in a way that ensures others understand your value. It's about owning your narrative and not waiting for someone else to tell your story or decide your worth.

Self-promotion is how you make your work visible, your voice heard, and your leadership felt.

And truthfully, people do it all the time. The difference is, some are rewarded for it while others are told to "stay humble." But humility doesn't mean invisibility. You can be humble and still be seen. You can be gracious and still be credited. You can be collaborative and still claim your success.

Promoting yourself doesn't mean pretending to be perfect. It means making sure your contributions aren't ignored, downplayed, or claimed by someone else.

This is important because, as mentioned in the previous chapter, you have mentors and you have monitors. And truthfully, there are more monitors than mentors. If you don't speak up for yourself, others in that specific scenario may not. Monitors aren't there to advocate for you, they're there to observe, often in silence, and sometimes in sabotage.

Think about how social media works. Promotion is everything. When you post content that shows value, confidence, and consistency, people respond. Engagement increases. Followers grow. The same applies professionally. When you promote yourself and can back it up, your support increases. Your "likes" become real-life endorsements and suddenly, you find yourself with options, opportunities, and moves to make.

Self-promotion isn't about being loud. It's about being clear. If you don't claim your space, someone else will fill it or worse, erase it altogether.

When I Promoted Myself into the Role I Wanted

When I felt it was time to transition into a Regional Vice President role, I didn't wait for someone to tap me on the shoulder. I positioned myself for the opportunity I believed I was ready for.

I started by researching companies I respected. Companies with solid reputations, strong leadership, and values that aligned with mine. I asked myself the same questions I mentioned back in Chapter 1. I looked at job descriptions for RVP roles, assessed where I stood, and pushed self-doubt to the side.

I didn't just want the job, I prepared for it.

I took a few classes to strengthen my financial acumen. I updated my professional online profile to reflect my qualifications. I reached out to people working at the companies I admired and asked to connect so I could ask informed questions. I sent cover letters, polished my resume, and showed up to local industry chapter meetings and professional engagements.

I followed up with every person who gave me a business card not once, but consistently. And over time, I filtered through those connections, learning who was worth maintaining relationships with, not based on who could offer me a job, but on who genuinely aligned with my growth. Many of them fell into the monitor category and I moved on.

Two years later, I was offered the very position I had been working towards. Not because someone handed it to me but because I claimed it. Interestingly enough, I was interviewed twice. The first time, they said no. That didn't stop me. I stayed in touch, continued networking and kept a positive attitude.

I made a plan, invested in myself, and promoted my value loud enough for the right people to hear and consistent enough for them to remember. It worked. They reached out and offered me a role that had been created specifically for me because they were impressed by how I carried myself. That's the power of self-promotion, self-awareness, and letting go of self-doubt. You have the power to shape your own future but only if you're bold enough to claim it.

Self-Promotion Checklist: Say It. Show It. Repeat It.

Want to promote yourself without losing your authenticity? Here's a simple checklist to keep you grounded and intentional:

- Know Your Value. Write down your key wins, skills, and what sets you apart then revisit them often.

- Update Your Presence. Keep your professional online presence, resume, and bio fresh. Don't wait until you need them.
- Speak with Substance. Talk about your results, not just your responsibilities. Quantify your impact.
- Find the Right Platforms. Share your insights at meetings, in newsletters, at panels, or through posts.
- Practice the Pitch. Be ready to explain who you are and what you bring confidently, concisely.
- Follow Up. After events or meetings, reconnect. Relationships grow with intentional follow-through.
- Be Consistent. Don't wait for a big moment. Promote yourself in small, steady ways that reflect your growth.
- Protect Your Narrative. Don't let others define your story. Own it. Shape it. Share it.

Your voice is powerful. Your presence is earned. And your success should never be a secret so speak up, stand out and always stay ready.

Chapter 7 Claiming Your Space – The Art Of Self-Promotion- Self Reflection

1. What stories are you not telling about your accomplishments and why?

2. When was the last time you confidently claimed your work in front of others?

3. How can you promote your value in a way that feels authentic, not performative?

4. What internal beliefs need to shift for you to step fully into your power?

Chapter 8

Empathy is often defined as the ability to understand and share the feelings of another. But I like to think of it more intimately: "Your pain in my heart."

Empathy isn't just about sympathy or good intentions. Rather, it's about presence. It's the ability to sit with someone's experience, feel it through their eyes, and respond not from ego, but from care. It's about stepping outside of your world and walking a few miles in someone else's even when their journey looks nothing like yours.

In leadership, empathy is everything.

It's the difference between issuing orders and offering support.

Between being in charge and being trusted.

Between managing people and truly leading them.

When you take the time to truly understand what someone is going through and what pressures they carry, what insecurities they hide, what dreams they chase, you become a different kind of leader. One who doesn't just correct behavior, but cultivates potential. One who doesn't assume, but asks. Who doesn't just react but responds.

Through active listening, you uncover not just surface problems, but the root needs. And once you know what someone truly needs, you can customize your care packet, your support, your feedback, your resources, all in a way that's personal, powerful, and transformative.

Because people don't just need direction, they need to be seen. They need to feel safe, respected, and valued. And when you show up as a person, you earn the right to show up as their leader.

When Leadership Requires More Than a Title

In my current role, I met a young woman who was, to put it lightly, rough around the edges. She was the assistant property manager at the time and was already in a position of leadership but struggling to carry it with care or professionalism.

Her appearance was far from corporate. Her grooming was unpolished, her clothing didn't align with traditional workplace expectations, and her tone regardless of the subject was always confrontational. You could feel her guard up before she ever said a word. Her energy said "I've survived a lot so don't test me."

Her very presence made people uncomfortable. The way she addressed residents often yelling, using politically incorrect language, and dismissing concerns left me stunned. It wasn't just unprofessional; it was abrasive, loud, and unfiltered.

But I didn't show up to judge her.
I showed up to understand her.
And more importantly, to understand what shaped her.

I began by simply spending time at the property. I conducted 100% unit inspection walking every unit, leaving no stone unturned. She walked those units with me.

That's where I started to hear the stress behind the sharpness.
To see the weight behind the walls she had built.

This wasn't just a tough property, it was a war zone disguised as a community. Half the day was spent removing members of the homeless population from stairwells. Maintenance staff regularly cleaned up urine, drug paraphernalia, and the remnants of overnight drug frenzies. It was not a safe place to work or live.

Police were called often. They came, they left, and the cycle restarted. The residents, exhausted and terrified, became vigilantes trying to take back their community with their own hands. Fights broke out. Tensions ran high.

Drug dealing was rampant. Shootings weren't rare. They were expected.

And in the middle of it all stood a young woman trying to earn a living.

How could she display anything but aggression?

How could she lead with calm, when every day demanded defense? How could she express empathy, when she never received any herself?

That's when I realized that she didn't need criticism, she needed care. She didn't need correction, she needed compassion with accountability.

I sat her down after the inspections were complete. I looked her in the eye and told her: You have truly championed for this property. I acknowledged what she had been up against, and how much strength it took just to show up each day.

Then I invited her to share her thoughts.

I asked her what she believed the property needed. What changes she thought could help make it better. What support she'd never been given. I told her we would look at it together and figure out how to implement what was possible.

And in that moment, something shifted.

The sparkle in her eye told me everything. It revealed the person behind the armor. Someone who wanted better, but didn't know how. Someone who had never been told she could lead with vision instead of volume.

We weren't at odds anymore. We were partners. Collaborators. Change agents.

Together, we created a long-term action plan. Over the next two years, we worked side by side to transform the property from a place of fear into a place of hope.

We partnered with local advocacy groups. We worked closely with the police department to create consistent, community-based enforcement strategies. We upgraded surveillance systems, installed secure access points, and implemented heavy monitoring protocols with random sweeps. We shared our plans with the authorities and made sure they were aligned with us. Most importantly, we stayed consistent. It took time, but it worked.

That community went from being the example of a place deemed hopeless to becoming the example of what is possible when people are given the resources, support, and leadership they deserve.

The young woman I met on day one? She received several promotions. Eventually, she was offered a powerful new opportunity. Before she left, she gave me a beautifully written letter of appreciation. A true heartfelt thank you for believing in her when she didn't even believe in herself.

She is no longer the person I met at the start.

She is someone who has shed her armor. Someone who now mentors' others. Someone who speaks with purpose instead of pain.

She continues to rise like the beacon she always was and now finally believes herself to be.

Empathy Isn't Excusing—It's Empowering

It's important to say this clearly: Empathy is not an excuse for harmful behavior. It's not about avoiding accountability. It's about creating space for understanding, so the response can match the reality.

When people are struggling, they often show symptoms before they even realize they're asking for help. What we interpret as attitude may actually be anxiety. What we call laziness may be burnout. And what appears as defiance may be exhaustion or fear.

Empathetic leadership doesn't mean lowering standards. It means lifting people toward them with clarity, care, and support.

You can be kind and still have high expectations. You can give grace and still set boundaries. One doesn't cancel out the other.

The Ripple Effect of Leading with Empathy

Empathy doesn't just transform individuals. It changes systems.

Once the tone shifted on that property, everything changed.

Residents began to feel safer. They trusted the leadership.

Maintenance and office staff morale improved.

Police and advocacy groups complimented our efforts.

The company itself began to point to that property as a turnaround story.

All because one leader refused to write someone off and chose, instead, to reach in.

How to Practice Empathy in Leadership.

Empathy isn't a trait you either have or don't. It's a practice. A skill. One that can be developed with intention.

Here are a few ways to lead with empathy:

- Ask before assuming. Instead of jumping to conclusions, ask: "Is everything okay?" or "What would help you right now?"
- Practice non-verbal listening. Put down your phone. Make eye contact. Give people your full attention.
- Pause before correcting. Ask yourself: "What might they be dealing with that I can't see?"
- Reflect progress, not just mistakes. Catch people doing things well. Name their growth. Reinforce the good.
- Coach, don't just command. When offering feedback, focus on developing their strengths not just fixing their flaws.

Empathy won't always be easy. But it will always be necessary.

Because sometimes, people don't need you to fix them. They need you to believe in the version of themselves they've never seen.

And when you do that, when you lead from that place, everything changes.

Chapter 8 Leadership With Empathy – Rising By Lifting Others- Self Reflection

1. How has someone's empathy (or lack of it) shaped your professional path?

2. Think of a time you led with empathy. What impact did it have on others—and on you?

3. What does it mean to lead without ego in your current role?

4. How can you model strength while still being human?

Chapter 9

They say to "climb the ladder," but sometimes the ladder is broken, blocked, or bolted to the ground. Sometimes, it's not about climbing straight up. It's about moving strategically across until the right door opens.

This chapter is about that truth.

It's about what happens after the storm. After the self-doubt. After the microaggressions, the leadership lessons, the moments you almost gave up. It's about taking everything you've been through not just as trauma, but as training. Turning experience into elevation. Hardship into strategy. Pain into positioning.

Shattering the glass ceiling doesn't always mean being handed the title. It means knowing you earned it even if they won't say it out loud.

And sometimes, making a lateral move isn't a step back. It's a sidestep to save your peace. A repositioning to protect your purpose. A calculated shift that gives you room to grow somewhere that sees you clearly.

How I Got Here: Lessons from the Climb

Every chapter before this one wasn't just a story, it was a stepping stone. A brick in the foundation of who I've become as a leader, a woman, and a professional who refused to be boxed in or broken down.

Instead of recapping each chapter in a list, I created this visual map to show the progression from survival to strategy to success.

From Surviving to Shattering Ceilings

This chart captures the transformation:

Each stage I passed through, the mindset shift that came with it and the outcome that empowered my next move

Every box represents a lesson learned, not given. These shifts didn't happen all at once. They were lived, wrestled with, and ultimately owned.

Topic	Challenge	Mindset Shift	Empowering Outcome
Surviving	Navigating difficult situations	I can adapt and persevere	Resilience in the face of adversity
Stability	Securing a firm foothold	I can create a strong foundation	Confidence in my position
Strategy	Capitalizing on opportunities	I can act with purpose and vision	Advancement through calculated action
Success	Attaining a key goal	I can reach new heights	Personal and professional fulfillment
Empowerment	Supporting others' growth	I can lift others as I rise	Leadership and positive impact

Now, with these lessons under my belt, I want to explore what it really looks like to shatter ceilings while also making strategic lateral moves. The kind that protect your peace and position you for your next rise.

The Ceiling Was Never Glass—It Was Concrete

The term "glass ceiling" makes it sound like you can at least see through it. Like what's blocking you is invisible, fragile, maybe even delicate.

But let's be real. In many workplaces, the ceiling is not glass. It's concrete. Reinforced. Unspoken. Guarded. And often, no matter how qualified or high-performing you are, you still find yourself stuck beneath it.

You get passed over while training the person who gets promoted. You watch opportunities go to those with less experience, but more "connection."

You raise your hand and somehow, you're still not called on.

Shattering that ceiling doesn't happen with one big swing. It happens with pressure, persistence, proof and yes, sometimes it happens by walking away from it entirely and finding another path that takes you higher even if it starts sideways.

That's what lateral moves are about.

Lateral Doesn't Mean Less

We've been conditioned to see progress as a straight vertical line. But real success especially for women, and especially for Black and Brown professionals, rarely moves that way.

Sometimes the most powerful move you can make isn't up, it's *out*.

A lateral move isn't a failure. It's not "settling." It's strategy.

It might mean stepping into a new company culture that values you.

It might mean entering a role that doesn't pay more (yet), but gives you peace and purpose as well as a real opportunity to grow.

It might mean switching lanes entirely so you can build experience in another department, expand your network, or recover from burnout without falling behind.

I've made lateral moves and every time, it gave me leverage.

The title didn't change. But my mindset did.

The salary didn't skyrocket, but the opportunities did.

The environment improved, and I could finally breathe again.

Because sometimes, peace *is* the promotion.

How You Know It's Time to Shift

No one hands you a sign that says, "It's time to go." More often, it shows up in subtle ways:

You stop being excited to share your ideas because you know they won't be heard.

You feel more like a placeholder than a contributor.

You're praised publicly but overlooked privately.

You leave work physically present but emotionally absent.

You start doubting your brilliance because no one around you reflects it back.

When that happens or if it's happening, you have a choice.

You can stay and try to crack the ceiling open from underneath, or you can shift laterally, reposition yourself, and find a space where your voice isn't just tolerated but valued.

That's not quitting. That's redirecting.

It's making a conscious decision to move where the energy aligns, where the potential expands, and where your growth isn't constantly met with resistance.

You don't owe any workplace your exhaustion.

You don't need to explain why you're ready for more.

You don't need to wait for a promotion to validate what you already know:

You are qualified.

You are capable.

And sometimes, you have to move sideways to rise on your own terms.

A Call to Action.

You have always been enough.

It's not that you couldn't handle it. It's that they wanted to contain your power in a box. They wanted your brilliance to fit into a mold that was never built for you. But here's the truth:

Don't shrink yourself so others can grow.

There is enough room at the table for everyone to flourish.

Focus on your growth. Invest in your elevation and while you're climbing, be intentional about who you keep around you. Determine who your mentors are and who your monitors are but be precise in sifting out the wheat from the weeds.

The next move you make should affirm your value not make you question it. It should align with your peace, your purpose, and your power. Because glass ceilings were never designed for you to live beneath.

They were made to be shattered.

Chapter 9 Shattering Ceilings And Making Lateral Moves- Self Reflection

1. What ceilings have you encountered that felt more like concrete than glass?

2. Describe a lateral move you made—or considered making. What did it teach you?

3. How do you define success now, compared to when you first started your career?

4. What needs to shift in your mindset or environment for your next elevation to occur?

Chapter 10

Success is complicated, especially when you navigate corporate America as a minority. Reaching the top often feels like you've overcome impossible odds. You've defied stereotypes, shattered expectations, and finally entered spaces that were historically inaccessible. Yet, with that achievement often comes unexpected, dangerous pressure, the subtle expectation to assimilate, to quietly conform, and to become a "silent partner" in maintaining the status quo.

Assimilation is seductive because it promises acceptance and belonging. It suggests that if you tone down your differences, blend in just enough, and avoid rocking the boat, you'll secure your hard-earned position. But assimilation, in reality, exacts a steep and deeply personal price. It encourages you to silence your authentic voice, abandon your advocacy, and ultimately become complicit in perpetuating the systems that once kept you locked outside.

It's disheartening to witness individuals succeed yet fail to support their teams or advocate for others' upward mobility. No one rises entirely alone; if your project succeeded, your team helped you get there. Don't forget that members of your team are seeking opportunities for growth as well.

I've witnessed talented, driven minorities reach senior roles and gradually transform from advocates into gatekeepers. Driven by fear and scarcity, the belief that there's only room for one, they become silent protectors of a flawed system. They embrace roles carefully crafted to meet diversity quotas and decide it's too much work to become a changemaker. Afraid to jeopardize their status, these individuals adopt behaviors and beliefs once wielded against them. Without realizing it, they've adopted the mindset of the very gatekeepers whose oppression they had to overcome.

The cost of assimilation isn't only personal; it's communal. When minorities who have reached success fail to lift others or speak against injustices, progress stalls. Opportunities remain scarce, and talented voices remain unheard. Assimilation fosters an environment where diversity is performative rather than transformative.

Breaking free of the assimilation trap requires courage. It demands rejecting comfortable silence in favor of active, purposeful advocacy. Real leadership doesn't blend in, it stands out, creating pathways for others. Real empowerment doesn't reinforce restrictive quotas, it dismantles them, building a broader, stronger foundation for future leaders.

Consider your position and influence carefully. Will you be a silent partner complicit in a quiet injustice, or will you harness your power to amplify marginalized voices, mentor emerging leaders, and challenge the system to genuinely embrace diversity?

The choice is stark, but the path forward is clear. Assimilation might offer temporary safety, but authenticity and advocacy build lasting legacies of empowerment and change.

Chapter 10 The Unshakable Spirit – Empowering Others Through Your Journey- Self Reflection

1. Who has helped you get to where you are, and how can you honor their investment in you?

2. What parts of your journey do you feel called to share—and with whom?

3. How are you currently mentoring or empowering someone else, formally or informally?

4. In what ways can your story be a source of healing or guidance for someone coming behind you?

Chapter 11

What good is wisdom if it dies with you?

That's the question I often ask myself when I reflect on the journey I've taken. The hard learned lessons, the emotional valleys, the strategies no one handed me but I had to fight to find.

If that experience isn't shared, who benefits?

When you hoard knowledge, you leave others to navigate the same storms without a compass. But when you pay it forward, you become the blueprint. The bridge. The living roadmap.

It's not enough to "make it." You have to reach back and make sure someone else does too.

Because humans? We're really not that different, especially those of us who've been overlooked, oppressed, or consistently underestimated. The moment we begin supporting one another instead of silently competing with one another, we become unstoppable.

Unity creates trust. Trust creates peace. And peace? That creates the kind of environments where everyone can rise.

Honoring Those Who Paved the Way.

The journey for these inventors was not paved with opportunity, it was filled with obstacles, resistance, and systemic erasure. Many of them had to navigate their own labyrinths, often without recognition, resources, or the protection of the law.

Some faced Patent discrimination, where their inventions were stolen or filed under someone else's name.

Some racial segregation, which denied them access to the very institutions that could fund or publish their work.

Others Financial gatekeeping, leaving them to bootstrap innovation with limited tools or support.

Don't forget social isolation, where their genius was either mocked, ignored, or attributed to others.

Despite these barriers, they pushed forward. They created. They innovated. They solved problems the world didn't even know it had yet.

And while their names aren't always included in history books, their legacy lives in every light bulb, traffic light, secure home, and medical breakthrough that traces back to their brilliance.

Too many minorities of the past paid it forward with their brilliance and never got the credit. Their contributions were stolen, renamed, or erased. But we remember.

Here are just a few Black inventors whose innovations shaped the world but whose stories too often go untold or vaguely remembered:

Lewis Latimer – Invented the carbon filament that made light bulbs last longer. I really believe that without him, Edison's design wouldn't have worked.

Madam C.J. Walker – Created a line of hair care products for Black women and became the first documented self-made woman millionaire in America.

Garrett Morgan – Invented the three-position traffic light and a precursor to the modern gas mask.

Marie Van Brittan Brown – Invented the first home security system, a design that led to the modern surveillance systems we use today.

Otis Boykin – Created electronic resistors used in everything from televisions to pacemakers.

Lonnie Johnson – A NASA engineer and inventor of the Super Soaker (which went on to generate over a billion dollars in sales).

These individuals were not just inventors, they were visionaries. Problem-solvers. Architects of progress.

A Final Word: Be the Spark

If there's one thing I hope this book leaves you with, it's this:

You are not alone on this path; you are part of a larger story. One built by those who dared to defy the odds, who shattered ceilings, who led with heart, and who left a trail of wisdom behind them so we wouldn't have to walk blindly.

Now it's your turn.

Share what you know. Speak your truth. Don't wait until you have the perfect platform. You are the platform. Every experience, every mistake, every success is part of the legacy you're building.

Don't hoard your light. Use it to ignite someone else's.

Because this world doesn't just need more leaders. It needs more liberators. People unafraid to lift others as they rise. People bold enough to leave the door open after walking through it. People with an unshakable spirit and a will to make sure that no one else has to start from scratch if you've already drawn the map.

Be the voice you once needed. Be the hand you once wished for. Be the spark someone else can follow.

And remember, your power was never meant to be contained. It was meant to be shared.

Chapter 11 The Unshakable Spirit – Empowering Others Through Your Journey- Self Reflection

1.Who has drawn a map that helped you navigate your professional path? Have you thanked or honored them?

2. What wisdom do you now carry that others could benefit from hearing?

3. How do you plan to "be the spark" for someone else this year?

4. What legacy do you want to leave behind in your family, your workplace, or your community?

Your Unshakable Goals

1. Embody Authentic Leadership
   I will lead with truth, empathy, and self-awareness, choosing presence over performance.
   Write how you will show up more authentically in your next leadership moment.

2. Protect My Peace While Pursuing Growth
   I will no longer sacrifice my well-being to prove my worth. I will set boundaries that honor both my ambition and my health.
   List one boundary you will create or strengthen...

3. Speak Up Even When It's Uncomfortable
   I will challenge microaggressions, bias, and disrespect with clarity and composure. Silence will no longer be mistaken for consent.
   Describe a situation where you will use your voice...

4. Invest in My Rise and Someone Else's
   I will mentor others while continuing to build my own path. I understand that my rise means nothing if I don't lift others with me.
   Name one person you will support and how...

5. Define Success on My Terms
   I will no longer chase titles, validation, or acceptance. I will define success through peace, purpose, and sustained impact.
   What does success look like for you today and not by their standard, but yours?..

6. Create Your Own Breakthrough Goal
   What other goals can you think of setting to bring out the best version of yourself? This is your invitation to name the transfor-

mation you still seek.

Write your custom goal down and how you plan to pursue it...

Final Thoughts

Keep Climbing, Keep Giving.

As you turn the final page of this book, I want to leave you with one last truth: you are not alone, and your journey is not in vain. Every challenge you've faced, every barrier you've broken, and every truth you've dared to speak has meaning. These are not just personal victories. They are stepping stones for someone else who is watching, learning, and following your lead.

My journey is still unfolding. As for me, I am still climbing the corporate ladder. I have not stopped. I continue to navigate new challenges, break new ground, and advocate for spaces where authenticity is valued over assimilation. This work is ongoing—not just for me, but for all of us.

So I encourage you to do the same. Pay it forward. Share your experiences. Mentor someone. Speak up even when your voice shakes. Because every time you extend your hand, you illuminate the path for someone else. And that is the true essence of being unshakable. Not just standing tall, but helping others rise too.

You are powerful. You are needed. And your story matters.

Stay rooted. Stay rising. Stay *unshakable.*

www.ingramcontent.com/pod-product-compliance
Lightning Source LLC
Chambersburg PA
CBHW071441210326
41597CB00020B/3895